KU-224-755

 www.heinemann.co.uk/library
Visit our website to find out more information about Heinemann Library books.

To order:
 Phone 44 (0)1865 888066
 Send a fax to 44 (0)1865 314091
 Visit the Heinemann Bookshop at www.heinemann.co.uk/library to browse our catalogue and order online.

First published in Great Britain by Heinemann Library,
Halley Court, Jordan Hill, Oxford OX2 8EJ, part of
Pearson Education.
Heinemann is a registered trademark of Pearson
Education Ltd.

Editorial: Kristen Truhlar and Diyan Leake
Design: Victoria Bevan and Tower Designs Ltd
Picture research: Mica Brancic
Production: Julie Carter

Origination: Dot Gradations
Printed and bound in China by South China
Printing Co. Ltd

ISBN 978 0 431 19148 5 (hardback)
12 11 10 09 08
10 9 8 7 6 5 4 3 2 1

ISBN 978 0 431 19154 6 (paperback)
13 12 11 10 09
10 9 8 7 6 5 4 3 2 1

British Library Cataloguing in Publication Data
Raum, Elizabeth
The history of the computer. - (Inventions that changed
the world)
1. Computers - History - Juvenile literature 2. Computers -
Social aspects - Juvenile literature
I. Title
303.4'834
ISBN-13: 9780431191546

Acknowledgements
The publishers would like to thank the following for
permission to reproduce photographs: p. 4 akg-images, p. 5
Getty Images/Hulton Archive, p. 6 Getty Images/Hulton Archive,
p. 7 Getty Images/Hulton Archive (Corbis/Bettman), p. 8 Topfoto,
p. 9 The Art Archive, p. 10 Science Photo Library/Los Alamos
National Laboratory, p. 11 Corbis/Bettman, p. 12 Getty
Images/Time & Life Pictures/Bob Peterson, p. 13 akg-images,
p. 14 Topfoto/The Image Works/Christopher Fitzgerald, p. 15
Corbis/Roger Ressmeyer, p. 16 Topfoto/The Image Works/Barry
Sweet, p. 17 Corbis/IBM, p. 18 Topfoto/Keystone, p. 19 Corbis/
Bettman, p. 20 Getty Images/Photographer's Choice/Marcus
Lyon, p. 21 Rex Features/Image Source, p. 22 Corbis/Galen
Rowell, p. 23 Alamy/ImageStage/Pictor International, p. 24
Science Photo Library/Hank Morgan, p. 25 Masterfile/Jon
Feingersh, p. 26 Alamy/Sally and Richard Greenhill, p. 27
Rex Features/Phanie/Burger.

Cover photograph of an IBM computer in the 1950s
reproduced with permission of Corbis/Hulton-Deutsch
Collection.

The History of the Computer

Elizabeth Raum

Heinemann
LIBRARY

Contents

Before computers 4

Help with numbers 6

The first computers 8

A computer as big as a house 10

Making computers better 12

Personal computers 14

Computer programs 16

A mouse helps out 18

Computers to take with you 20

The Internet 22

The World Wide Web 24

How computers changed life 26

Timeline 28

World map activity 29

Find out more 30

Glossary 31

Index 32

Some words are shown in bold, **like this**. You can find out what they mean by looking in the glossary.

Before computers

Today many people have computers in their homes. Everyone knows what a computer is. But 100 years ago, no one had even heard of a computer.

Before computers, people used an abacus to do maths.

People had to find other ways to do the work computers do now. They used an **abacus** to work with big numbers. They wrote letters by hand or with a **typewriter**. Then they took them to the post office to send them.

People used typewriters like this one to write letters.

Help with numbers

Without computers, people had trouble when they needed to work with huge numbers. Many **inventors** worked to make counting machines. In the United Kingdom, Charles Babbage worked on plans for machines that would help people with maths problems.

Charles Babbage is sometimes called "the Father of the Computer".

Herman Hollerith was a teacher. In 1884 he invented this counting machine.

In 1896 Herman Hollerith, who lived in the United States, started a company (now called IBM) to make **calculators**, or counting machines. The counting machine was very useful. But soon people were looking for something even better.

The first computers

It took time to make a real computer. In 1941 the United Kingdom and the United States were fighting a war against Germany. They hoped computers could help. In 1943 the Harvard Mark I computer was **invented** in the United States. It helped out with maths problems.

The first computers, like Harvard Mark I, did not have computer screens.

Many people worked on the Colosuss computer.

The Colossus computer was built in the United Kingdom in in the same year, 1943. The Colossus was the first **electronic** computer. The Colossus could read messages written in a secret **code**.

A computer as big as a house

Three years later, in the United States, John Mauchly and J. Presper Eckert built a better computer called ENIAC. ENIAC was fast. It took ENIAC 30 seconds to answer a hard maths problem. Without the computer, it took 12 hours.

The ENIAC computer was as big as a small house.

The UNIVAC computer was about the size of a bedroom.

Mauchly and Eckert kept building better computers. In 1951 they built a smaller computer called UNIVAC. UNIVAC could do many jobs. It helped count the number of people who lived in the United States.

Making computers better

The first computers had very little **memory**. This means that they could only store, or remember, about 1,000 words. **Inventors** worked to give computers more memory. Today's computers can store millions of words and numbers.

The first computers were big, but had little memory.

In the 1960s, people started using computers at work.

By the 1960s, inventors found ways to make computers smaller. Companies began buying computers to help with their work. Most computers could do only one job. Many were used to count big numbers.

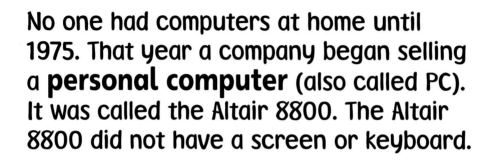

Personal computers

No one had computers at home until 1975. That year a company began selling a **personal computer** (also called PC). It was called the Altair 8800. The Altair 8800 did not have a screen or keyboard.

People could buy the Altair 8800 computer already put together, or they could put it together themselves. It took many hours to put together.

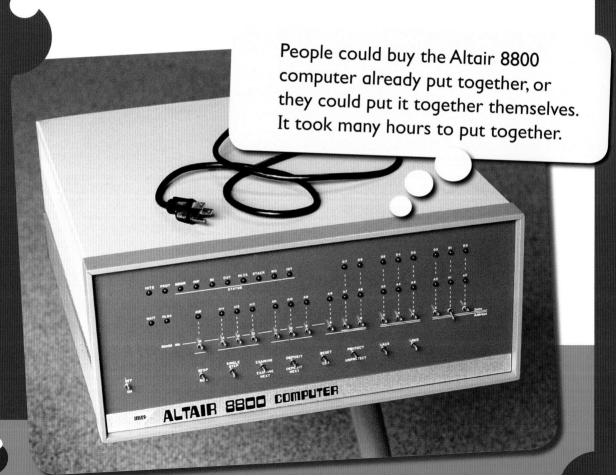

The first PCs could only do one job. The PCs did whatever they were built to do. Some did maths or played games. As more people bought PCs, they wanted computers to do many different things.

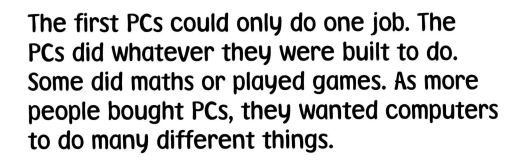
Some people used early home computers to play games.

Computer programs

In 1975 Bill Gates and Paul Allen, of the United States, **invented** a way to tell PCs what to do. They wrote **programs**. Programs told a computer what to do. If a computer had many programs, it could do many jobs.

In 1975 Bill Gates helped begin a company called Microsoft to make and sell computer programs.

This IBM computer from 1981 has a screen, keyboard, and printer.

IBM, the company started by Herman Hollerith, began selling computers that were already put together. These computers came with programs. They could do many jobs. Computers used programs to keep lists, type letters, and answer maths problems.

A mouse helps out

The first IBM PCs did not come with a mouse. In 1964 a man in the United States, Douglas Engelbart, **invented** the computer mouse. The first mouse was made of wood. The mouse made it easier to use a computer.

Douglas Engelbart called this a mouse because it was small and the wire looked like a tail.

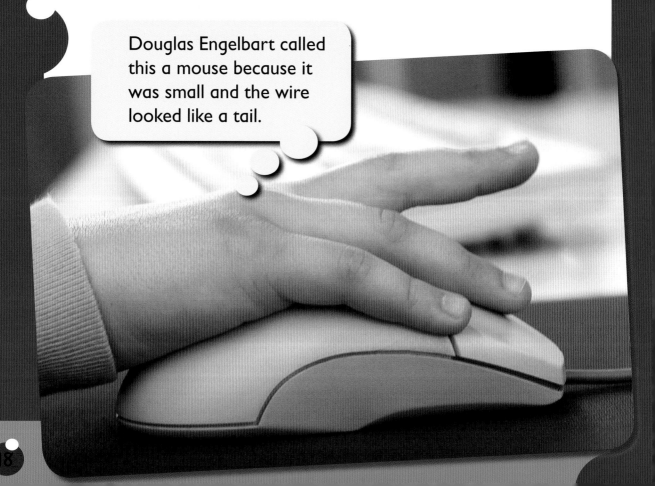

In 1976 Steve Jobs (left) and Steve Wozniak (right), both of the United States, started Apple Computers.

In 1984 a company called Apple Computers added a mouse to their computers. Soon other computers came with a mouse. People used the mouse to start up computer **programs**, move things on the screen, and play games.

Computers to take with you

In 1980 a man in the United Kingdom named William Moggridge made an even smaller computer. It was first used on a trip into space. By 1981 several companies began selling **laptop** computers. Laptops were small enough to carry from place to place.

Laptop computers are easy to take to school or work.

This handheld computer is so small that it can fit in a pocket.

Inventors made laptops better and better. Soon they weighed less, but had bigger screens. By 1993 computers were so small they could fit in a person's hand. A handheld computer is called a **PDA** (personal digital assistant).

The Internet

In the 1960s, **inventors** wanted to find a way that a computer in one place could work with a computer in another place. In 1969 the United States government came up with a plan to **connect** computers. They called the new plan the **Internet**.

The computers in this lab in the South Pole connect to computers far away by using the Internet.

Today computers can connect to the Internet from home, school, work, and many other places.

By 1986 the computers in 165 places were working together using the Internet. Most of the computers were in **universities**. At first, the Internet was not easy to use. Inventors wanted to find a better way to send words and numbers over the Internet.

The World Wide Web

In 1989 a man in the United Kingdom named Tim Berners-Lee made a special computer **program**. The program made it easier to send words and numbers over the **Internet**. He called his program the **World Wide Web** (also called www).

Tim Berners-Lee invented the World Wide Web.

Today people use the World Wide Web to send email messages and visit **websites**. In the year 2000, **inventors** had the new idea of sending radio and television shows over the World Wide Web. They called this a **podcast**. The first podcasts began in 2003.

People can watch podcasts on their computers.

How computers changed life

Today very few people use a **typewriter** or **abacus**. People use computers to answer maths questions, to write projects and letters, and to send email. Computers **connect** us to other people all over the world.

People in schools use computers to learn things.

Today doctors and nurses use computers to help people.

Today computers have many uses. School children use computers to learn. Doctors use computers to make people well. People find new ways to use computers every day.

Timeline

1884 Herman Hollerith **invents** an electric counting machine.

1943 Harvard Mark I and Colossus are invented.

1946 ENIAC computer is built.

1951 UNIVAC computer is built.

1964 Douglas Engelbart invents the mouse.

1969 United States government sets up the **Internet**.

1975 First **PCs** are made.

1975 Bill Gates and Paul Allen invent computer **programs**.

1984 Apple Company includes a mouse with a computer.

1989 Tim Berners-Lee invents the **World Wide Web**.

1993 Handheld computers (PDAs) are invented.

2003 First **podcasts** are sent to computers.

World map activity

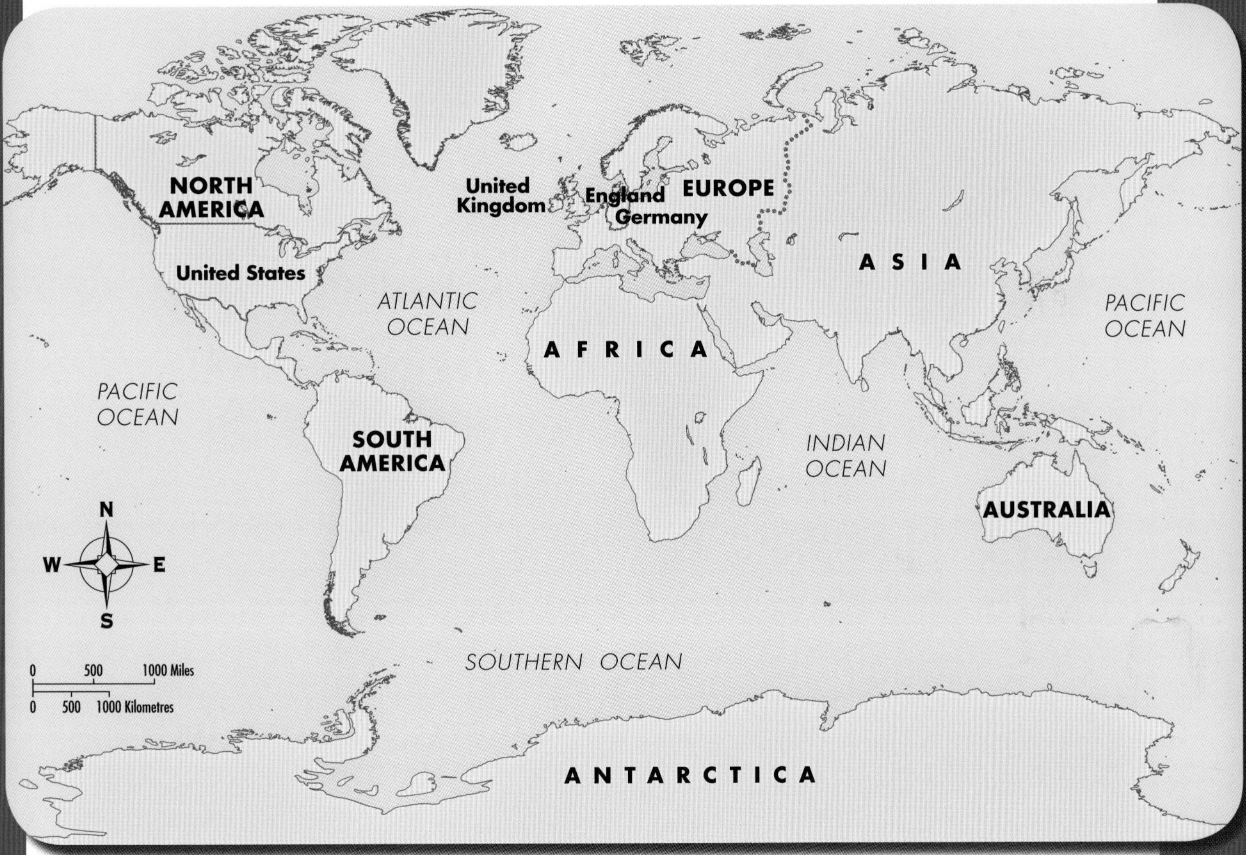
NORTH AMERICA
United States
United Kingdom
England
Germany
EUROPE
ASIA
ATLANTIC OCEAN
PACIFIC OCEAN
AFRICA
PACIFIC OCEAN
SOUTH AMERICA
INDIAN OCEAN
AUSTRALIA
N
W
E
S
0 500 1000 Miles
0 500 1000 Kilometres
SOUTHERN OCEAN
ANTARCTICA

The countries talked about in this book are labelled on this world map. Try to find each **inventor**'s country on the map.

Find out more

Books

High-Tech Inventions, Gerry Bailey (Mercury, 2005).

My First Computer Guide, Chris Oxlade (Heinemann Library, 2007).

The Picture History of Great Inventors, Gillian Clements (Frances Lincoln, 2000).

Websites

Enchanted Learning – http://www.enchantedlearning.com/inventors

Technology at Home – http://www.pbs.org/wgbh/aso/tryit/tech

Glossary

abacus frame with sliding beads used to solve number problems

calculator machine that adds, subtracts, multiplies, and divides

code secret message

connect put together

electronic something that uses electricity

Internet system that connects computers

invent make something that did not exist before

inventor someone who makes something that did not exist before

laptop computer that folds up and can be taken places

memory way a computer stores numbers and words

PDA (personal digital assistant) handheld computer

personal computer (PC) computer people use at home

podcast radio or TV show sent over the internet

program something that tells a computer what to do

typewriter machine people used to write letters before there were computers

university place where older students carry on with their education

websites pages on the World Wide Web

World Wide Web (www) program that lets people send email and visit websites

Index

abacus   4-5, 26
Allen, Paul   16
Altair 8800   14
Apple   19

Babbage, Charles   6
Berners-Lee, Tim   24

calculators   7
Colossus   9
connecting computers   22-23

Eckert, J. Presper   10-11
electric counting machine   7
electronic computer   9
email   25, 26
Engelbart, Douglas   18-19
ENIAC   10

games   15
Gates, Bill   16
Germany   8

Harvard Mark I   8
Hollerith, Herman   7

IBM   7, 17, 18
Internet   22-23, 24

Jobs, Steve   19

laptop computer   20-21

maths   8, 13, 15
Mauchly, John   10-11
memory   12
Moggridge, William   20
mouse   18-19

personal computer (PC)   14-15,
      16, 18
personal digital assistant (PDA)
      21
podcasts   25
programs   16-17, 19, 24

typewriter   5, 26

United Kingdom   8, 9, 20, 24
United States   6-7, 8, 10-11,
      16, 18-19, 23
UNIVAC   11

websites   25
World Wide Web (WWW)   24-25
Wozniak, Steve   19